About the Marine Sanctuaries Conservation Series

The National Oceanic and Atmospheric Administration administers the National Marine Sanctuary Program. Its mission is to identify, designate, protect and manage the ecological, recreational, research, educational, historical, and aesthetic resources and qualities of nationally significant coastal and marine areas. The existing marine sanctuaries differ widely in their natural and historical resources and include nearshore and open ocean areas ranging in size from less than one to over 5,000 square miles. Protected habitats include rocky coasts, kelp forests, coral reefs, sea grass beds, estuarine habitats, hard and soft bottom habitats, segments of whale migration routes, and shipwrecks.

Because of considerable differences in settings, resources, and threats, each marine sanctuary has a tailored management plan. Conservation, education, research, monitoring and enforcement programs vary accordingly. The integration of these programs is fundamental to marine protected area management. The Marine Sanctuaries Conservation Series reflects and supports this integration by providing a forum for publication and discussion of the complex issues currently facing the National Marine Sanctuary Program. Topics of published reports vary substantially and may include descriptions of educational programs, discussions on resource management issues, and results of scientific research and monitoring projects. The series facilitates integration of natural sciences, socioeconomic and cultural sciences, education, and policy development to accomplish the diverse needs of NOAA's resource protection mandate.

M/V *CONNECTED*
Coral Reef Restoration Monitoring Report
Monitoring Events 2004-2005
Florida Keys National Marine Sanctuary
Monroe County, Florida

Joe Schittone
Erik C. Franklin
J. Harold Hudson
Jeff Anderson

Florida Keys National Marine Sanctuary
National Marine Sanctuaries Program, National Ocean Service
National Oceanic and Atmospheric Administration

U.S. Department of Commerce
Carlos M. Gutierrez, Secretary

National Oceanic and Atmospheric Administration
VADM Conrad C. Lautenbacher, Jr. (USN-ret.)
Under Secretary of Commerce for Oceans and Atmosphere

National Ocean Service
John H. Dunnigan, Assistant Administrator

Silver Spring, Maryland
December 2006

National Marine Sanctuary Program
Daniel J. Basta, Director

REPORT AVAILABILITY

Electronic copies of this report may be downloaded from the National Marine Sanctuaries Program web site at http://www.sanctuaries.noaa.gov/. Hard copies may be available from the following address:

National Oceanic and Atmospheric Administration
National Marine Sanctuary Program
SSMC4, N/ORM62
1305 East-West Highway
Silver Spring, MD 20910

COVER

Upper left: *Acropora palmata* colony on Western Sambo Reef near the M/V *Connected* restoration site, Florida Keys National Marine Sanctuary. Photo credit: Jeff Anderson. Lower right: Reef crown (#86), photographed on July 12, 2004, from the M/V *Connected* restoration site, Florida Keys National Marine Sanctuary. Photo credit: Jeff Anderson.

SUGGESTED CITATION

Schittone, J., Franklin, E.C., Hudson, J.H., Anderson, J. 2006. M/V *Connected* Coral Reef Restoration Monitoring Report, Monitoring Events 2004-2005. Florida Keys National Marine Sanctuary Monroe County, Florida. Marine Sanctuaries Conservation Series NMSP-06-10. U.S. Department of Commerce, National Oceanic and Atmospheric Administration, National Marine Sanctuary Program, Silver Spring, MD. 25 pp.

CONTACT

Joe Schittone, corresponding author, at: Joe.Schittone@noaa.gov

ABSTRACT

This document presents the results of the monitoring of a repaired coral reef injured by the M/V *Connected* vessel grounding incident of March 27, 2001. This grounding occurred in Florida state waters within the boundaries of the Florida Keys National Marine Sanctuary (FKNMS). The National Oceanic and Atmospheric Administration (NOAA) and the Board of Trustees of the Internal Improvement Trust Fund of the State of Florida, ("State of Florida" or "state") are the co-trustees for the natural resources within the FKNMS and, thus, are responsible for mediating the restoration of the damaged marine resources and monitoring the outcome of the restoration actions. The restoration monitoring program tracks patterns of biological recovery, determines the success of restoration measures, and assesses the resiliency to environmental and anthropogenic disturbances of the site over time.

The monitoring program at the *Connected* site was to have included an assessment of the structural stability of installed restoration modules and biological condition of reattached corals performed on the following schedule: immediately (i.e., baseline), 1, 3, and 6 years after restoration and following a catastrophic event. Restoration of this site was completed on July 20, 2001. Due to unavoidable delays in the settlement of the case, the "baseline" monitoring event for this site occurred in July 2004. The catastrophic monitoring event occurred on August 31, 2004, some 2 ½ weeks after the passage of Hurricane Charley which passed nearby, almost directly over the Dry Tortugas. In September 2005, the year one monitoring event occurred shortly after the passage of Hurricane Katrina, some 70 km to the NW. This report presents the results of all three monitoring events.

KEY WORDS

Florida Keys National Marine Sanctuary, coral, grounding, restoration, monitoring, Hurricane Charley, Hurricane Katrina, *Acropora palmata*

TABLE OF CONTENTS

LIST OF FIGURES AND TABLES

ACKNOWLEDGEMENTS

The National Oceanic and Atmospheric Administration (NOAA) and the Board of Trustees of the Internal Improvement Trust Fund of the State of Florida, ("State of Florida" or "state") are the co-trustees for the natural resources within the FKNMS and, thus, are responsible for mediating the restoration of the damaged marine resources and monitoring the outcome of the restoration actions. The authors would like to express their appreciation to all Florida Department of Environmental Protection employees who participated in the initial response, damage assessment, restoration, and case settlement associated with this vessel grounding.

INTRODUCTION

This document presents the results of the monitoring of a repaired coral reef injured by the M/V *Connected* vessel grounding incident of March 27, 2001. This grounding occurred in Florida state waters within the boundaries of the Florida Keys National Marine Sanctuary (FKNMS). The National Oceanic and Atmospheric Administration (NOAA) and the Board of Trustees of the Internal Improvement Trust Fund of the State of Florida, ("State of Florida" or "state") are the co-trustees for the natural resources within the FKNMS and, thus, are responsible for mediating the restoration of the damaged marine resources and monitoring the outcome of the restoration actions. The restoration monitoring program tracks patterns of biological recovery, determines the success of restoration measures, and assesses the resiliency to environmental and anthropogenic disturbances of the site over time. To evaluate restoration success, reference habitats adjacent to the restoration site are concurrently monitored to compare the condition of restored reef areas with "natural" coral reef areas unimpacted by the vessel grounding.

The monitoring program at the *Connected* site included an assessment of the structural stability of installed restoration modules and biological condition of reattached corals, which was to have been performed on the following schedule: immediately (i.e., baseline), 1, 3, and 6 years after restoration and following a catastrophic event (Table 1). Restoration of this site was completed on July 20, 2001. Due to unavoidable delays in the settlement of the case, the "baseline" monitoring event for this site occurred on July 12-13, 2004. Hurricane Charley (August 2004), which passed almost directly over the Dry Tortugas, triggered the post-catastrophic monitoring event, which occurred on August 31, 2004. In 2005, Hurricanes Dennis and Katrina, the later of which passed the site about 70 km to the NW, transpired before a monitoring effort at the site could be mounted. However, the site was visited shortly after the passage of Hurricane Katrina, with the monitoring event occurring in mid-September 2005.

Table 1. Event timeline for the M/V *Connected* grounding site; assessment, restoration, and monitoring.

Event	Date
Vessel Grounding	March 27, 2001
Assessment: Initial	March 27, 2001
Assessment: Aerial photography	April 5, 2001
Assessment: Number of coral fragments counted	April 25, 2001
Restoration	June 20-July 20, 2001
Baseline Monitoring	*July 12-13, 2004*
Post-catastrophic Monitoring	August 31, 2004
Year One Monitoring	September 13,2005
Year Three Monitoring	Summer 2007
Year Six Monitoring	Summer 2010

Damage Assessment

[Note: The information in this section was adapted from the Discussion section of the _Connected_ _Vessel Grounding Assessment_ prepared by Lauri J. MacLaughlin and William B. Goodwin]

The _Connected_, a 59.9-foot motor vessel, struck and damaged the shallow reef crest at Western Sambo reef, located south of Boca Chica Key on March 27, 2001 (Figure 1). The predominant coral species observed among the injured area was the elkhorn coral _Acropora palmata_ (Lamarck, 1816; Figure 2). Other coral species present included mustard hill coral (_Porites astreoides_), lettuce coral (_Agaricia agaricites_), fire coral (_Millepora complanata_), golfball coral (_Favia fragum_) and starlet coral (_Siderastrea siderea_). Other living components of the injured area included crustaceans, macroalgae, sponges, echinoderms, mollusks, octocorals and fish.

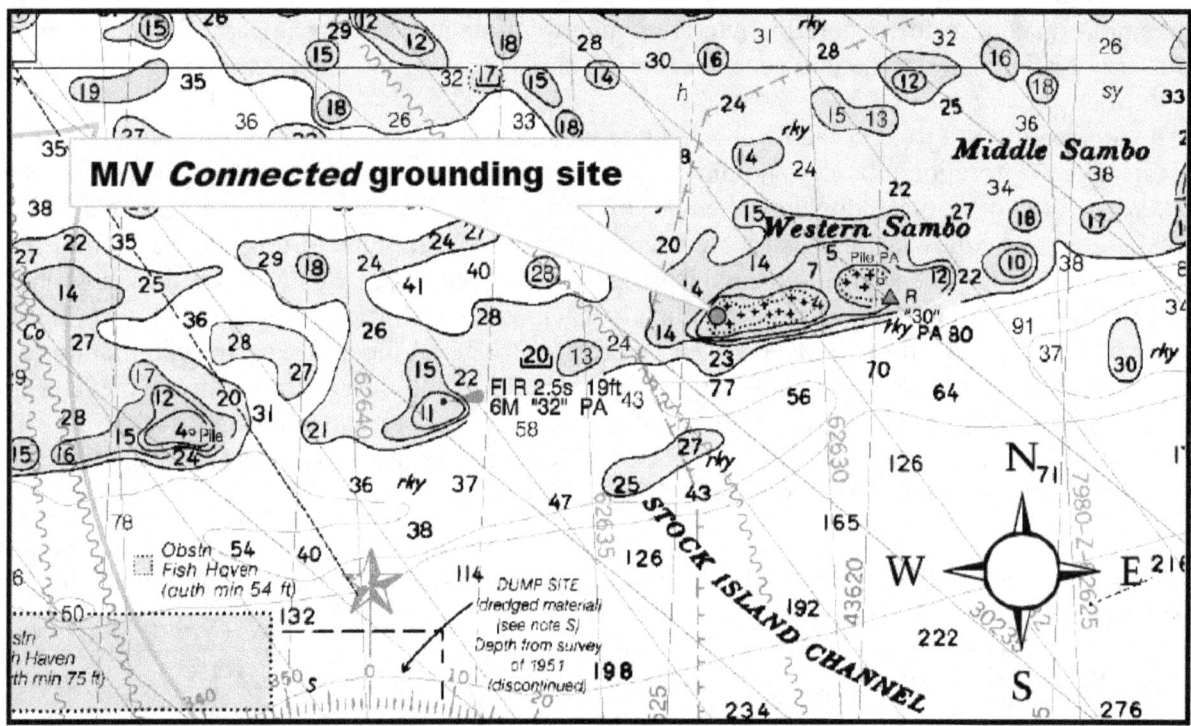

Figure 1. Approximate location (shown on NOAA Chart 11442) that the M/V _Connected_ ran aground on the reef crest of Western Sambo Reef on March 27, 2001.

The most prominent feature of the injury site consisted of a wide grounding track plowed through an elkhorn coral stand (Figure 2). The width of the injury swath varied between 3-7 m along the inbound path and widened at the final resting place to 9 m (Figure 3). The latitude and longitude of the beginning of the inbound track were recorded as 24° 28.811' N and 81° 43.105' W and the end of the inbound track as 24° 28.822' N and 81° 43.091' W (datum GRS80). During removal, the vessel was pivoted and extracted to the south (Figure 3). The area of damaged reef framework and live coral colonies from the inbound path and resting place was 189.58 m^2. In addition, small intermittent areas of injury were documented in front of the

2

inbound path (4.02 m^2), near the bow resting place (0.64 m^2), and adjacent to the pivot point (8.24 m^2). The total length of injury was 81.2 m and the total area of injury was 202.48 m^2 of reef framework and corals, predominately the elkhorn coral *Acropora palmata*.

Figure 2. Elkhorn coral, *Acropora palmata*, the predominant coral species of the shallow reef crest habitat, damaged by the M/V *Connected* grounding at Western Sambo Reef (photo credit: Bill Goodwin, FKNMS).

Coral Reef Restoration

[Note: The information in this section was adapted from the <u>M/V *Connected* Grounding Site Habitat Restoration at Western Sambo Reef in the Florida Keys National Marine Sanctuary</u> prepared by Marine Resources Inc.]

The objectives of the M/V *Connected* site restoration were to 1) provide lost habitat structure, 2) salvage and reattach displaced coral fragments, and 3) stabilize reef substrate along the impact track. To accomplish these objectives, three hundred seventy coral fragments were reattached within and to the exterior of twenty "reef crown" restoration modules (numbered 80-99) installed along the vessel's track and resting place (Figure 4). The fragments were irregularly shaped and ranged between 20-100 cm along their longest axis.

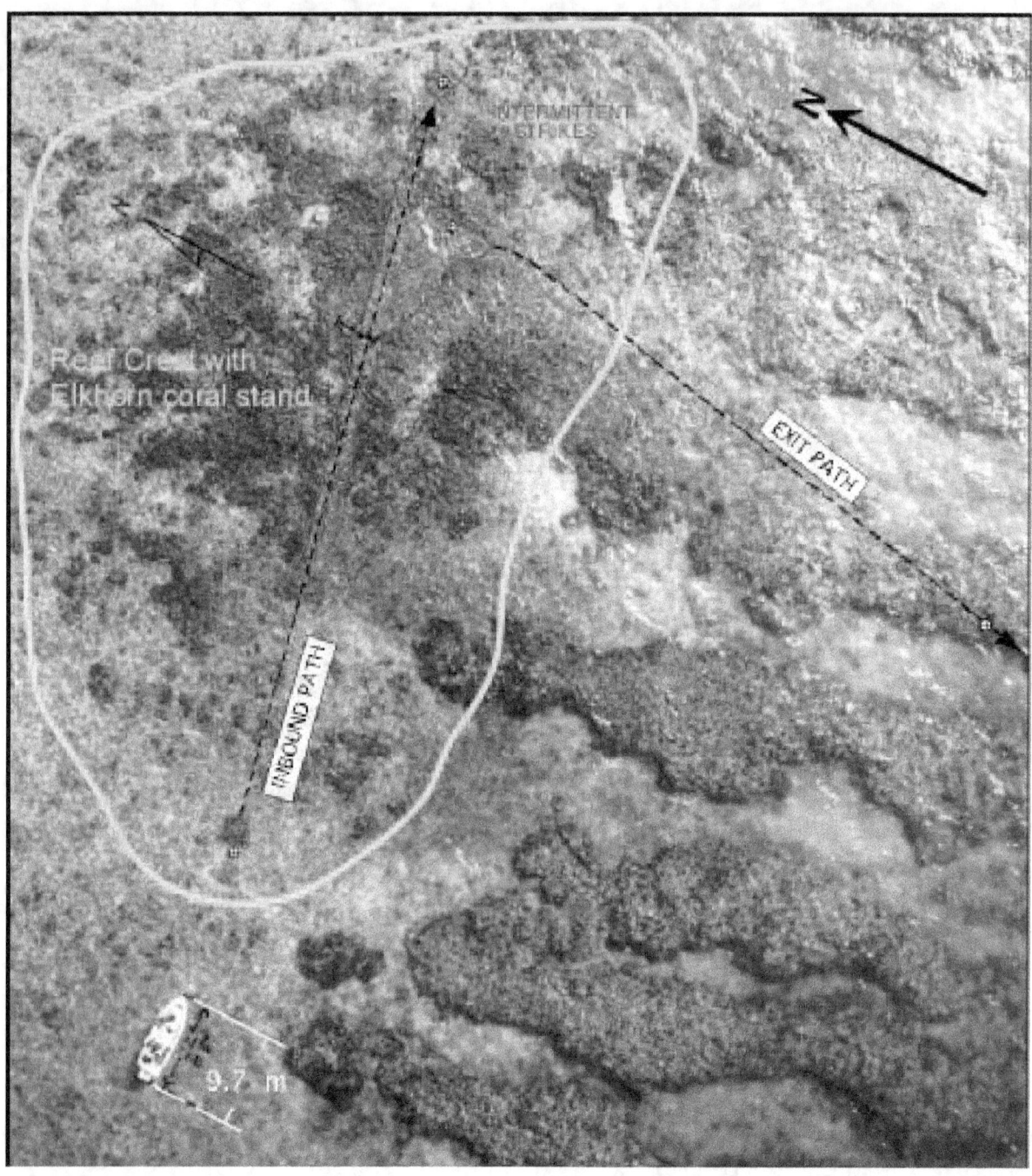

Figure 3. The M/V *Connected* grounding site at Western Sambo Reef with the area damaged from the vessel's inbound path and final resting place outlined in red. The aerial photograph was taken on April 5, 2001.

4

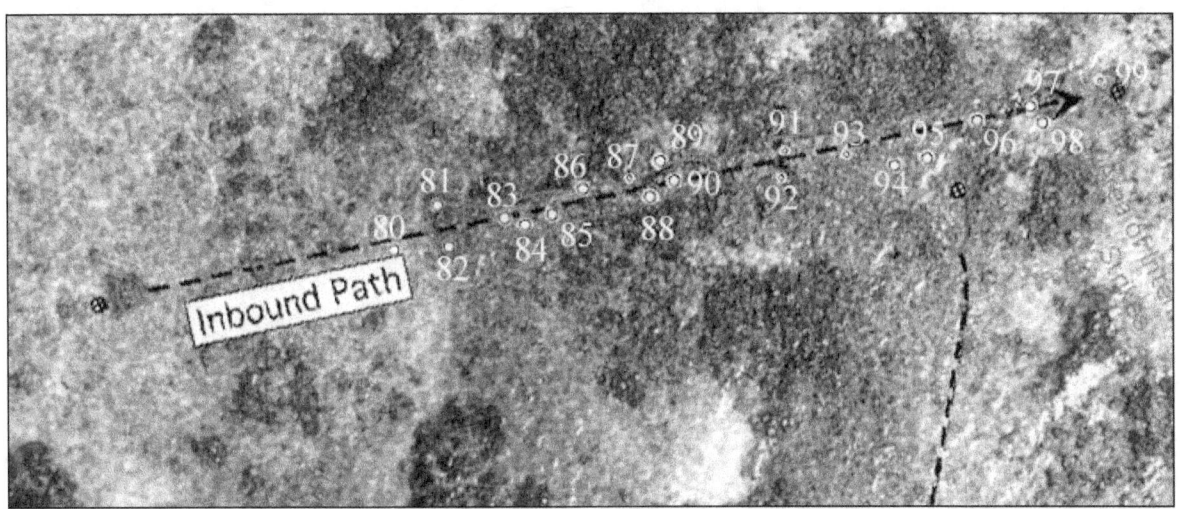

Figure 4. Diagram of reef crown restoration modules (white circles) installed at the *Connected* grounding site (inset from Figure 3). Large circles are "king crowns" and small circles are "queen crowns."

To meet the restoration objectives of the site, "reef crowns" (Figure 5) were proposed to anchor a group of damaged reef fragments and elevate them off of the seafloor. The reef crowns would stabilize the disturbed reef substrate and salvaged coral tissue and enhance the physical relief of the damaged area. The cylindrical structures were created with Portland type II cement, sand, limestone rock aggregate, topped by limestone rocks, and anchored to the substrate with iron reinforcing rods. Short-length (15cm) fiberglass reinforcing rods were used to ensure structural integrity of cement layers with modules. Two sizes of reef crowns were installed; fifteen modules were 1.2 m (outer) diameter rings ("king crowns") and five modules were 0.9 m (outer) diameter rings ("queen crowns"). Coral fragments were stabilized within the center of the modules with a layer of Portland cement-based grout (Figure 6).

Project oversight was provided by Harold Hudson, FKNMS, with the restoration performed by Marine Resources, Inc. (MRI). Field operations by MRI during the habitat restoration were conducted using a 9-m (30-ft) MAKO® vessel with sufficient deck space to allow transport of reef replacement modules and to accommodate SCUBA and construction equipment. A 5-m (16-ft) Carolina Skiff® with minimal draft was used during specialized vessel operations along the impact track. On-board navigation during transit to and from the project site was achieved using a Furuno® differential global positioning system (DGPS).

Locations of reef crowns along the impact track were selected by Harold Hudson, FKNMS, prior to their placement. Reef crowns were deployed along the impact track using lift bags and/or a specialized flotation platform. Reef crowns deployed using lift bags were transported by vessel to an area directly west of the impact track and launched overboard onto the sand/rubble bottom substrate. They were subsequently moved underwater to the pre-selected location utilizing the equivalent of a 300-lb lift bag and a bridle array. Other reef crowns were launched overboard while securely attached to the flotation platform and subsequently deployed from the flotation platform directly onto the pre-selected location. Reef crowns were placed on patches of firmly consolidated reef substrate along the impact track that were relatively devoid of attached reef biota. Most sand and loose debris within the inside opening of the reef crown was removed and small voids between the hard substrate and the module were filled with reef substrate fragments prior to coral reattachment. Fiberglass (5/8-inch) and/or metal rebar (¾-inch) was placed into the substrate within the opening of the reef crowns prior to coral reattachment to provide sheer strength and matrix reinforcement. Following reef crown placement and preparation, a grout mixture of approximately 1 part Portland type II cement to 1 part sand was made for filling the inside opening of the module and reattaching corals. Grout was prepared utilizing a Gilson® 6.5 ft³ mixer. Buckets of grout were transported by divers to the reef crowns and tightly packed into the opening to ensure filling voids within the substrate as well as between the substrate and the structure. Fragments of reef substrate devoid of coral tissue were pressed into the grout mixture to augment fill. Cached hard coral fragments within the impact track and occasional loose corals found outside the impact track were set into the grout mixture, once the structure was filled approximately to a height slightly above structure wall. Hard coral fragments were reattached within the reef crown opening in a manner that closely resembles the natural distribution of the existing habitat. The grout fill was smoothed and graded to slightly slope away from the center of the full module to prevent trapping sediment. Grout was also placed along the outside edge of the reef crown at locations of visible voids between the structure and substrate to prevent scouring and subsequent undercutting. Reef substrate and coral fragments were attached as "dressing" to the outer vertical surface of the reef crown to enhance aesthetic quality of the restoration.

Cross-section and Plan view of Reef Crown

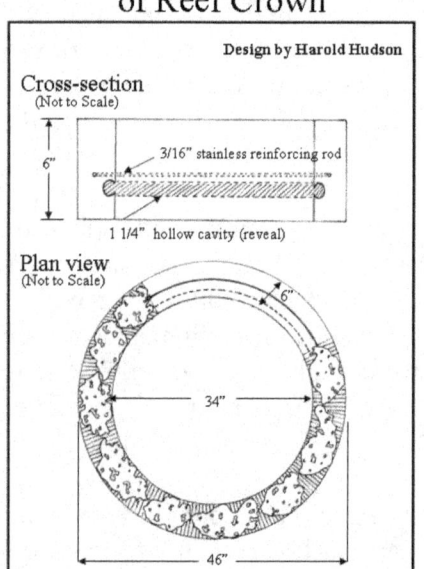

Cross-section of Installed Reef Crown

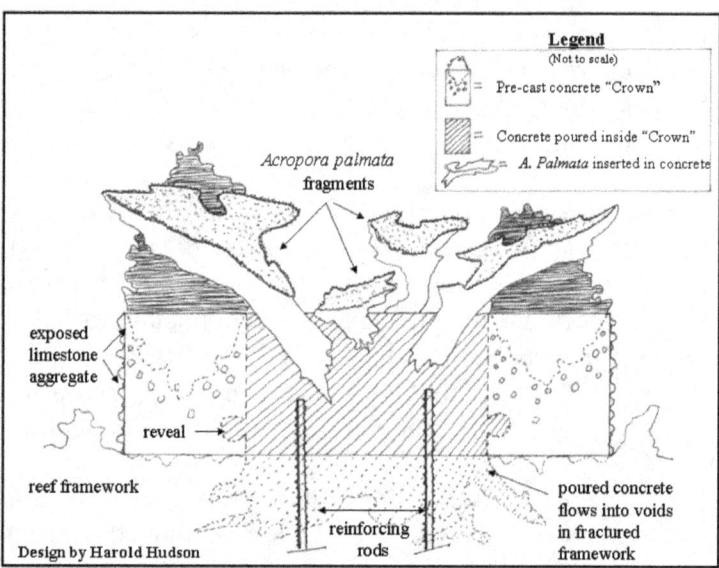

Figure 5. Cross-section and plan views of "Reef Crowns," as designed, and artist's conception of an installed crown.

Figure 6. A "king crown" restoration module installed on seafloor prior to addition of coral fragments to center of the module.

Restoration Monitoring

The purpose of the coral restoration monitoring program is to evaluate the success of trustee actions in achieving restoration goals and to determine if remedial measures are needed. For a grounding site such as the M/V *Connected*, the evaluation of restoration efforts involves the identification of appropriate success criteria and the design and implementation of a sampling and analysis plan. A list of success criteria measures for structural and functional aspects of coral reef restoration as well as a framework for monitoring activities is identified by NOAA (Thayer et al. 2003).

The guiding hypotheses for the evaluation of the "restoration" site reflects the efficacy of the restoration techniques and the condition of the site relative to reference habitats. The monitoring program addresses if the chosen restoration methods are effective and when the site could be considered restored. The structural integrity of the restoration site is evaluated with the following questions:

1. Is the attachment of the reef crowns to the substrate stable?
2. Are there any visible cracks in the surface of the reef crowns?
3. Is there any visible physical damage to the reattached coral colonies?

In addition, the biological condition of the restoration site was evaluated with the following question:

Is there a difference in coral cover between the grounding site (i.e., both the restored and unrestored areas) and the reference area?

The monitoring program was designed to detect significant changes in coral cover or damage to restoration components (structural enhancements, coral transplants, etc.) as a result of external events, such as major storms or vandalism, and in comparison to the surrounding habitat. In addition, the monitoring assessed the effectiveness of the restoration based upon technical evaluation of appropriate parameters.

METHODOLOGY

BASELINE MONITORING EVENT (JULY 2004)

Field Methods

On July 12-13, 2004, the *Connected* restoration site was monitored using SCUBA from a small vessel (6.4 m). Tactile and visual assessments were performed to evaluate the physical stability of the reef crowns. To determine the biological condition of the site, *in situ* observations, digital images, and digital videos were recorded among the restoration area and the reference area. The restoration area was composed of the 20 reef crowns (area = 20 m^2) and the remaining damaged, but unrepaired section of the grounding site (area = 182 m^2). The reference area was adjacent to the north side of the grounding path and similar in size (i.e., 202 m^2) and shape to the restoration area. Within each area, twenty 1 m^2 quadrats were surveyed for coral cover, corallivorous snail density and the presence of coral disease, coral bleaching, and damselfish. In addition, all twenty reef crowns were surveyed with 1 m^2 quadrats. Within the unrepaired section of the restoration area and the reference area, the location of quadrat placements were randomly chosen from a digital grid of uniquely identified 1 m^2 cells overlain on the grounding site map. In the field, transect lines were used from landmarks to determine cell locations as best as possible. Quadrats were deployed to these cells and visually surveyed for biological variables of interest.

Planar digital photographs of quadrats were recorded when depth allowed while oblique digital photographs and dGPS coordinates (with a Garmin 76) were taken of each restoration module in the restored area. Underwater digital images were collected with an Olympus C-5050 digital camera in a Light & Motion Tetra 5050 underwater housing and digital videos were collected with a Sony DCR-DVD200 video camera in an Amphibico QuickView DVD underwater housing.

Photo Analysis

Digital images were edited with Adobe Photoshop version 7 (Adobe 2002). Image edits included color hue changes to make water look bluer, brightness changes to compensate for original exposure, and sharpness changes to enhance images not in focus. Planar images of quadrats were corrected using the Panorama Tools plug-in for Photoshop to correct for barrel distortion of the extreme wide angle image making it as close to square as possible. Finally, excess image information outside the quadrat boundary was cropped.

Data Analysis

Data analysis and visualization were performed on a Dell PC with Statistica version 6 (StatSoft 2003) and Microsoft® Excel 2002 software. Basic descriptive statistics were generated for samples collected among the restoration, reference, and damaged unrestored areas.

POST-CATASTROPHIC MONITORING EVENT (AUGUST 2004)

On August 13, 2004, hurricane Charley passed just to the east of the Dry Tortugas. Maximum gusts recorded at the Key West airport were 58 mph. In order to see how the storm affected the restoration, a catastrophic monitoring event was undertaken on August 31. Methodology utilized was identical to that related above.

Data collection revealed that the site was not statistically significantly different from its condition during the baseline monitoring, seven weeks previously. In fact, the data indicated that coral cover was very slightly greater at the August monitoring event for all three categories: the reef crowns, the damaged unrestored area, and the reference area. However, the differences were so slight as to be encompassed by anticipated sampling distribution variance, as reflected by the standard error of the means. Therefore, the August 2004 monitoring coral cover percentages will be used in the figures and text which follow.

YEAR ONE MONITORING EVENT (SEPTEMBER 2005)

Another monitoring event occurred on September 13, 2005. Methodology utilized was identical to that related above for the previous two monitoring events.

Between the catastrophic (Aug. 2004) and the year-one (Sep. 2005) monitoring events, two powerful hurricanes passed within less than 100 kilometers of the restoration site; Dennis in July, and Katrina in August 2005. (Those familiar with last year's hurricanes in the region might remember that hurricanes Rita and Wilma did likewise, but both these were after the 2005 monitoring event.)

Results of the baseline, catastrophic, and 2005 monitoring are presented in summary fashion below. Complete copies of the datasets are maintained by both the FKNMS monitoring team, and by NMS headquarters Damage Assessment and Restoration Program staff.

RESULTS

BASELINE MONITORING EVENT (JULY 2004)

Structural Integrity

The baseline monitoring occurred in July 2004, three years after the restoration, at which time the stability and surface of all 20 restoration modules were found to be visually and tactilely sound. The modules were found in place with a stable attachment to the substrate and no visible cracks in the cement surface. There was no noticeable physical damage to the reattached coral fragments. In addition, *Acropora palmata* fragments among several modules had overgrown the cement interface and coalesced their tissue in the center of the module ring (see photos in APPENDIX).

Biological Condition

The *Connected* restoration site contained a matrix of solitary live *Acropora palmata* colonies, live *A. palmata* thickets, dead *A. palmata* skeletons, and reef rubble. Coral species observed within quadrats included *Acropora palmata*, *Agaricia agaricites*, *Diploria clivosa*, *Favia fragum*, *Millepora alcicornis*, and *Porites asteriodes*. *Acropora palmata* was the dominant coral species and represented 96% of the reported coral cover. Reflecting the habitat matrix of the reef flat, samples of coral cover within areas were heterogeneous; cover ranged from 0% to 59% in the restoration area and from 0% to 58% in the reference area. Unfortunately the contractor who did the restoration in 2001 did not establish a reference area, so there was no possibility of determining the trajectory of corals surrounding the grounding site, at least as of the time of the baseline monitoring. In 2004, mean coral cover was approximately 8% in the damaged unrestored area and 19.5% in the reference area. The coral cover of the reef crowns was estimated as 34% (Figure 7). Accompanying vertical growth, representing increased topographic complexity, can be assessed from the photos (see photos in APPENDIX).

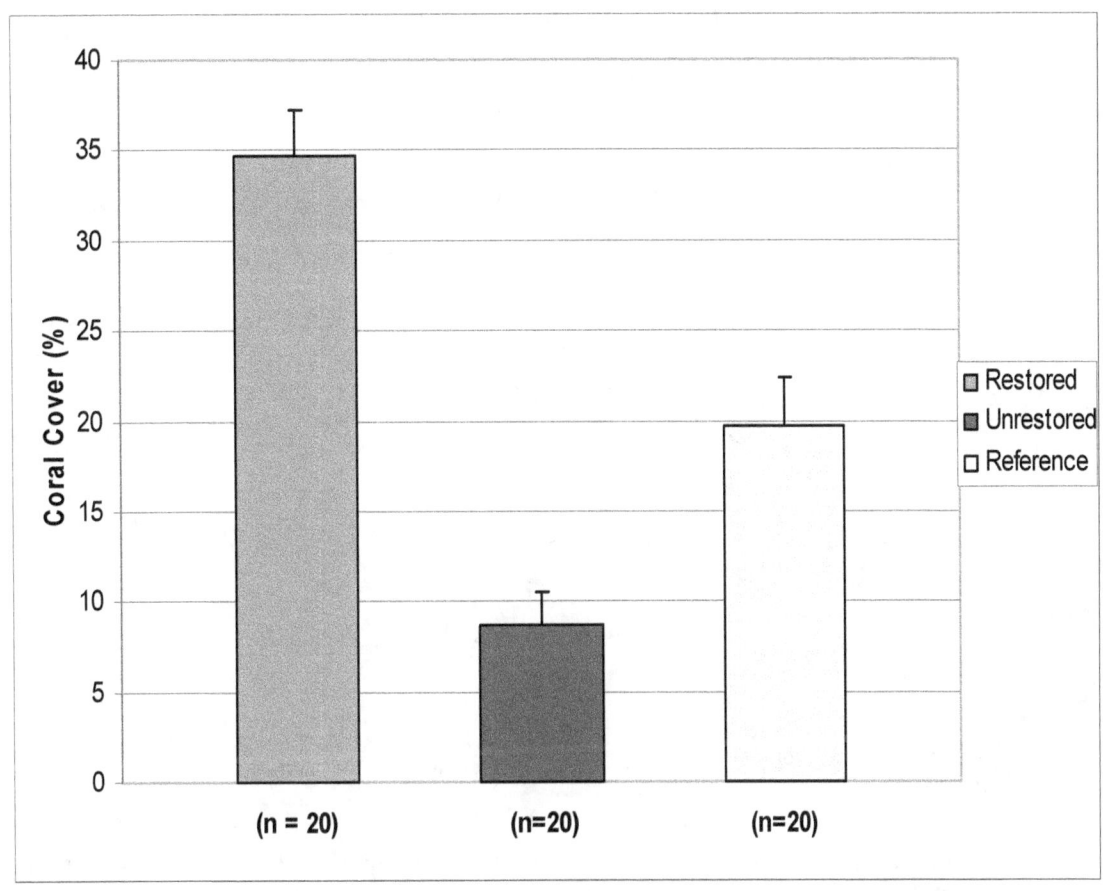

Figure 7. 2004 — mean (±SE) coral cover (%) among the restored (reef crown) area, the damaged unrestored area, and the reference area of the *Connected* grounding site.

In August 2001, shortly after the restoration was completed, a series of near-vertical underwater digital photographs were taken of the reef crowns. Using a random point count method software (Kohler 2004), coral cover was estimated as 16% in 2001 from 50 points per photo frame. Therefore, utilizing the 2004 monitoring data, the coral cover of the reef crowns had increased approximately 6% per year (absolute coverage) since the restoration in 2001 (Figure 8).

Coral predators, coral disease, and damselfish were observed within the restoration site. The density of corallivorous snails (*Coralliophila* sp.) was 0.1 snails m^2 (8 individuals total) in the restoration area and no snails in the reference area. White pox was observed on *Acropora palmata* colonies in two quadrats on reef crowns but not in the reference area. White band disease and coral bleaching were not observed in either of the areas. Damselfish were observed among 20% of quadrats in the restoration and 25% of the reference area.

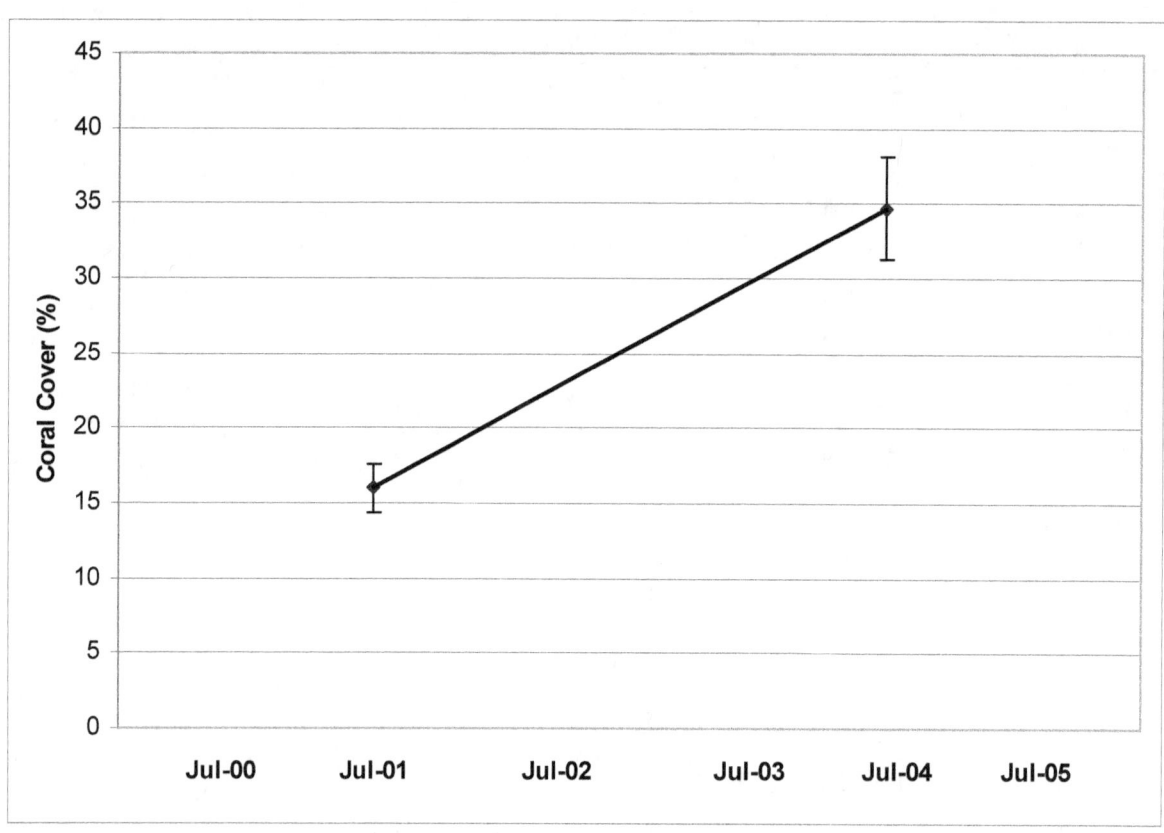

Figure 8. Trend in mean (±SE) coral cover (%) of the reef crowns of the *Connected* grounding site from 2001 to 2004.

POST-CATASTROPHIC MONITORING EVENT (AUGUST 2004)

Structural Integrity

Despite the near passage of hurricane Charley, the stability and surface of all 20 restoration modules were found to be visually and tactilely sound. However, as can be expected in a storm event, there was slight noticeable physical damage to a few reattached coral colonies. The tips of some fragments appeared to have been recently broken (e.g. reef crown #86; APPENDIX and Figure 9). Notice, at the time of this monitoring event, the "wound" is already being covered with algae and some coral tissue growth.).

Additional, non-storm-related structural damage was also documented (attributable to a boat strike), highlighting the multiple challenges faced at this site. The reef crown (#87; APPENDIX and Figure 9) is in relatively shallow water (~ 1.5 m), and the damage was very recent; perhaps a day or less old. This opinion is based on the fact that the wound did not have any signs of algae overgrowth, and fresh bottom paint was visible in the vicinity. The good news concerning the incident is that there was no visible damage to the reef crown module; thus the remaining living *Acropora palmata* tissue had a good chance to recover, absent intervening causes.

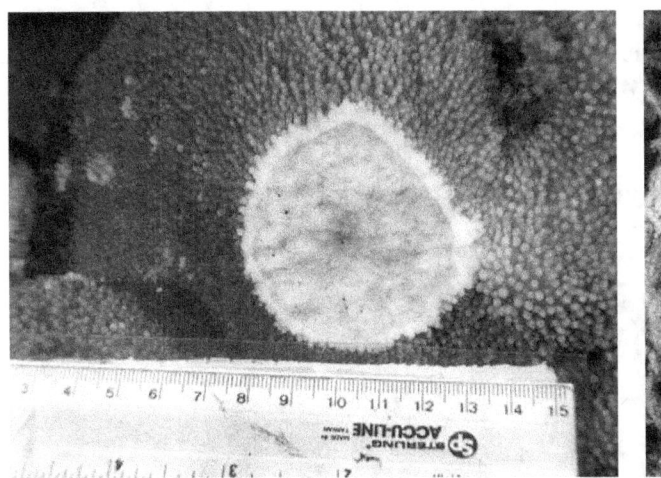

Figure 9. Broken branches on *Acropora palmata* colonies on reef crown #86 (left) and #87 (right).

Biological Condition

At this monitoring event, coral cover of all areas of the grounding site was statistically unchanged. Although some tissue abrasion damage and skeletal fragmentation were observed, the majority of reef crown colonies suffered either no or relatively minor injuries. Meanwhile, the reference area evidenced essentially no change from the baseline pre-Hurricane Charley monitoring event (July) to the immediately post-hurricane monitoring event (August).

YEAR ONE MONITORING EVENT (SEPTEMBER 2005)

Structural Integrity

As previously related, the Year One monitoring event was conducted on September 13, 2005. This was after the near passage of Hurricane Dennis in July, and Hurricane Katrina in August. The status of the site after the passage of one or the other (or possibly the combination of both) of these later hurricanes presented a different picture than was evidenced after Hurricane Charley the previous year. [Note: those familiar with the area will remember that Hurricanes Rita and Wilma also struck the vicinity in 2005; however, both these storms occurred after the year one monitoring event in September.]

The stability and surface of 19 of the twenty restoration modules were found to be visually and tactilely sound. One reef crown was dislodged from the substrate (Figure 10). Close inspection by the Sanctuary biologist, Harold Hudson, who was also present during the restoration of the site, determined that the module had been incorrectly installed with too few and too short sections of rebar securing it to the substrate. Other reef crowns (e.g. modules 83, 85, and 99 photos in APPENDIX), while still securely affixed, did have loose substrate eroded from their bases. This erosion can be directly traced to instability of the underlying substrate. Close inspection of the site revealed that instead of a well-cemented reef framework, the reef underpinning there was composed of loose *Acropora palmata* debris held in place by tightly-packed sediment. Washout of the stabilizing sediment by hurricane-driven waves resulted in the observed erosion at the bases of these reef crowns. Two other reef crowns (e.g. modules 91 and 92 photos in APPENDIX), still securely affixed to their locations in a natural depression in the reef, were completely buried by unconsolidated reef rubble.

Figure 10. Reef crown (#84) uprooted and overturned by storm-generated waves.

Biological Condition

As can be expected in a storm event, there was noticeable physical damage to some reattached *Acropora palmata* colonies. The tips of many fragments appeared to have been recently broken and other colonies showed signs of "sand blasting" (see photos in APPENDIX).

At the time of the 2005 monitoring, coral cover of the reef crowns was 22.2%. This was down approximately 36% from what cover had been the summer before (about 12% in terms of absolute cover). However, this pales in comparison to the damage done at the reference site, where cover was found to be 2.2%. This was reduced almost 89% (relatively) from the previous monitoring event (a reduction of ≈17.5% in absolute terms). A very similar degradation trend was observed at the damaged, unrestored site, where relative cover likewise decreased 88% (Table 2 and Figure 11).

Table 2. Reductions in coral cover between the 2004 catastrophic and 2005 monitoring events.

(All values are percentages)	Reef Crown Coral Cover	Reference Site Coral Cover	Unrestored Area Coral Cover
2004	34.7	19.7	8.7
2005	22.2	2.2	1.0
Reduction (relative)	36.0	88.6	88.0
Benthic Coral Cover Decrease (absolute)	12.5	17.5	7.7

The much greater reduction in coral cover in the reference zone can probably be attributable to the fact that most of the site lies below the bathymetry of the reef crowns; thus it served as a natural repository for the rubble and sediment which blanketed the whole area. This view is buttressed by the fact that damage (almost exclusively as a result of burial by storm-generated sediment) was differentially experienced among the reef crowns according to their elevation. For example, crowns which lay in a natural depression or "channel" were wholly smothered (e.g. reef crowns 91 and 92 in APPENDIX; these were buried in rubble which had to be excavated to ID the crowns for the photos.).

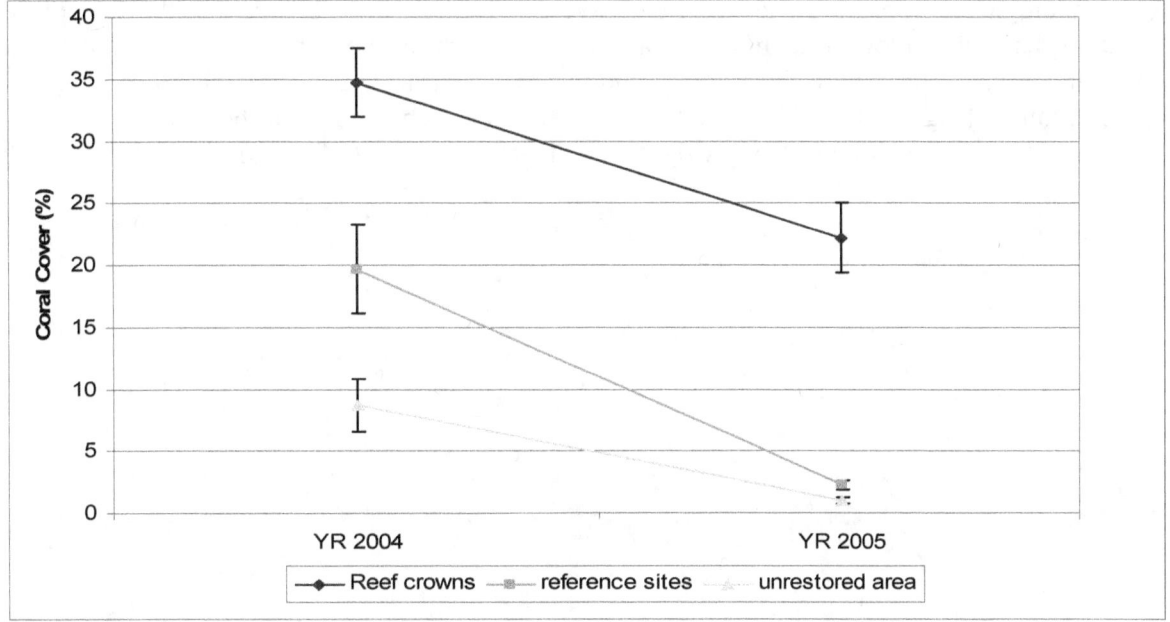

Figure 11. Trends in mean (±SE) coral cover (%) of the reef crowns, reference sites, and unrestored areas from 2004 to 2005.

SUMMARY

Monitoring suggests the reef crowns were an effective restoration methodology for facilitating the recovery of damaged *Acropora palmata* at Western Sambo reef, as evidenced by the first three years of the recovery process following restoration (Figure 8; APPENDIX). Nonetheless, given the extreme shallowness of this site, or any other site situated at such a similarly shallow depth, a restoration is unavoidably vulnerable to damage by the passage of a strong hurricane. The results documented by the FKNMS monitoring team impart a visually graphic, and easily comprehendible take-home lesson.

Comparison to the monitoring report regarding the M/V *Jacquelyn L* site (q.v., in the Sanctuaries' "Conservation Series"), which lies almost immediately adjacent to the *Connected* site, should prove informative. Although the groundings at the two sites were separated by a decade, the restorations took place only a year apart (*Jacquelyn L* in July 2000; *Connected* in July 2001). Thus the sites had 3 and 4 years respectively to establish themselves before the passage of Hurricane Charley in 2004, and 4 and 5 years before Hurricanes Dennis and Katrina in 2005 (with the *Jacquelyn L* site having the extra year). The much greater success enjoyed by the *Connected* restoration in both years, compared to the complete destruction of the *Jacquelyn L* site during the 2005 hurricane season, provides much in the way of valuable information and "lessons learned" to the Damage Assessment and Restoration Team of the National Marine Sanctuary Program. A restoration site should be elevated as much as possible, consistent with surrounding substrate contours. Any effort that can be made to get the coral fragments' "head out of the sand" is effort well spent. Even in the absence of near passage by a hurricane, isolating fragments to the extent practical from the usual scour caused by bottom currents, tides, surge, etc., will pay dividends in terms of tissue survival. After all, these small colonies are already experiencing stress from the incident which gave rise to their fragmentation in the first place. Anything that helps alleviate additional energy expenditure by the coral polyps attributable to sediment removal would be beneficial, and allow them to put energy into growth and reproduction. Along the same lines, loose rubble should be removed from the area, to prevent it from being launched as fragment-breaking "projectiles" in the event of a storm.

LITERATURE CITED

Adobe, Inc. 2002. Photoshop (image processing software), version 7. www.adobe.com.

Goodwin, W. B. and L. J. MacLaughlin. 2001. *Connected* vessel grounding assessment report. Confidential report prepared for NOAA General Counsel and FDEP Office of General Counsel. 2 pp. plus figures.

Kohler, K. E. 2004. CPCe - Coral Point Count with Excel extensions. Computer software. National Coral Reef Institute, Nova Southeastern University, Ft. Lauderdale, FL.

Marine Resources Inc. 2001. M/V *Connected* grounding site habitat restoration at Western Sambo Reef in the Florida Keys National Marine Sanctuary. Prepared for Fowler, White, Burnett, Hurley, Banick, and Strickroot. 8 pp. plus an appendix.

StatSoft, Inc. 2003. STATISTICA (data analysis software system), version 6. www.statsoft.com.

Thayer, G. W. , T. A. McTigue, R. J. Bellmer, F. M. Burrows, D. H. Merkey, A. D. Nickens, S.J. Lozano, P. F. Gayaldo, P. J. Polmateer, and P. T. Pinit. 2003. Science-based restoration monitoring of coastal habitats, volume one: A framework for monitoring plans under the Estuaries and Clean Waters Act of 2000 (Public Law 160-457). NOAA Coastal Ocean Program Decision Analysis Series No.23, Volume 1. NOAA National Centers for Coastal Ocean Science, Silver Spring, MD. 35 pp. plus appendices.

APPENDIX

Comparative photographs of reef crown restoration modules at M/V *Connected* grounding site on July 19, 2001 (photo credits: MRI, Inc.), July 12, 2004, August 31, 2004, and September 13, 2005 (photo credits: Jeff Anderson).

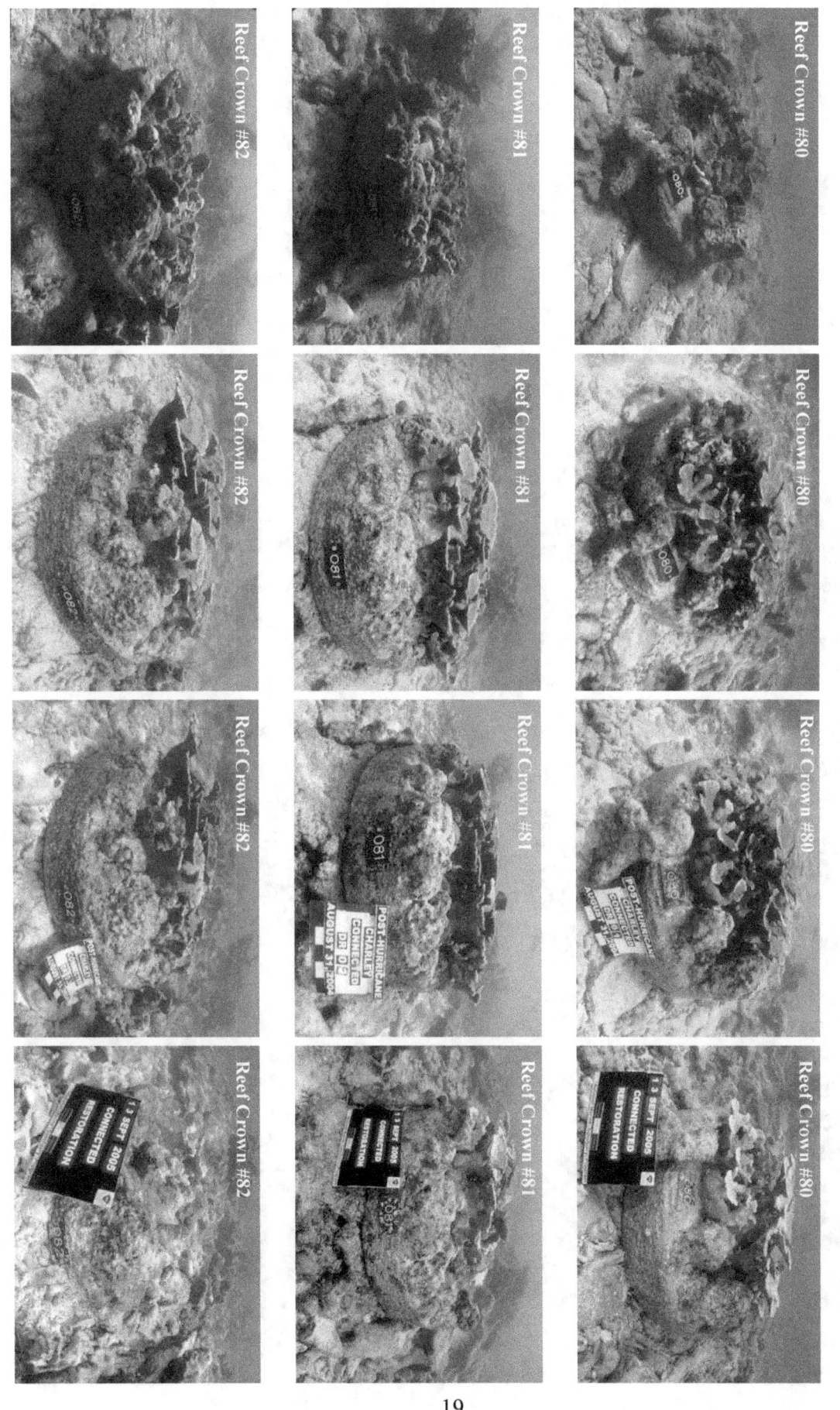

Reef Crown #83 — July 19, 2001
Reef Crown #84 — July 19, 2001
Reef Crown #85 — July 19, 2001

Reef Crown #83 — July 12, 2004
Reef Crown #84 — July 12, 2004
Reef Crown #85 — July 12, 2004

Reef Crown #83 — August 31, 2004
Reef Crown #84 — August 31, 2004
Reef Crown #85 — August 31, 2004

Reef Crown #83 — September 13, 2005
Reef Crown #84 — September 13, 2005
Reef Crown #85 — September 13, 2005

20

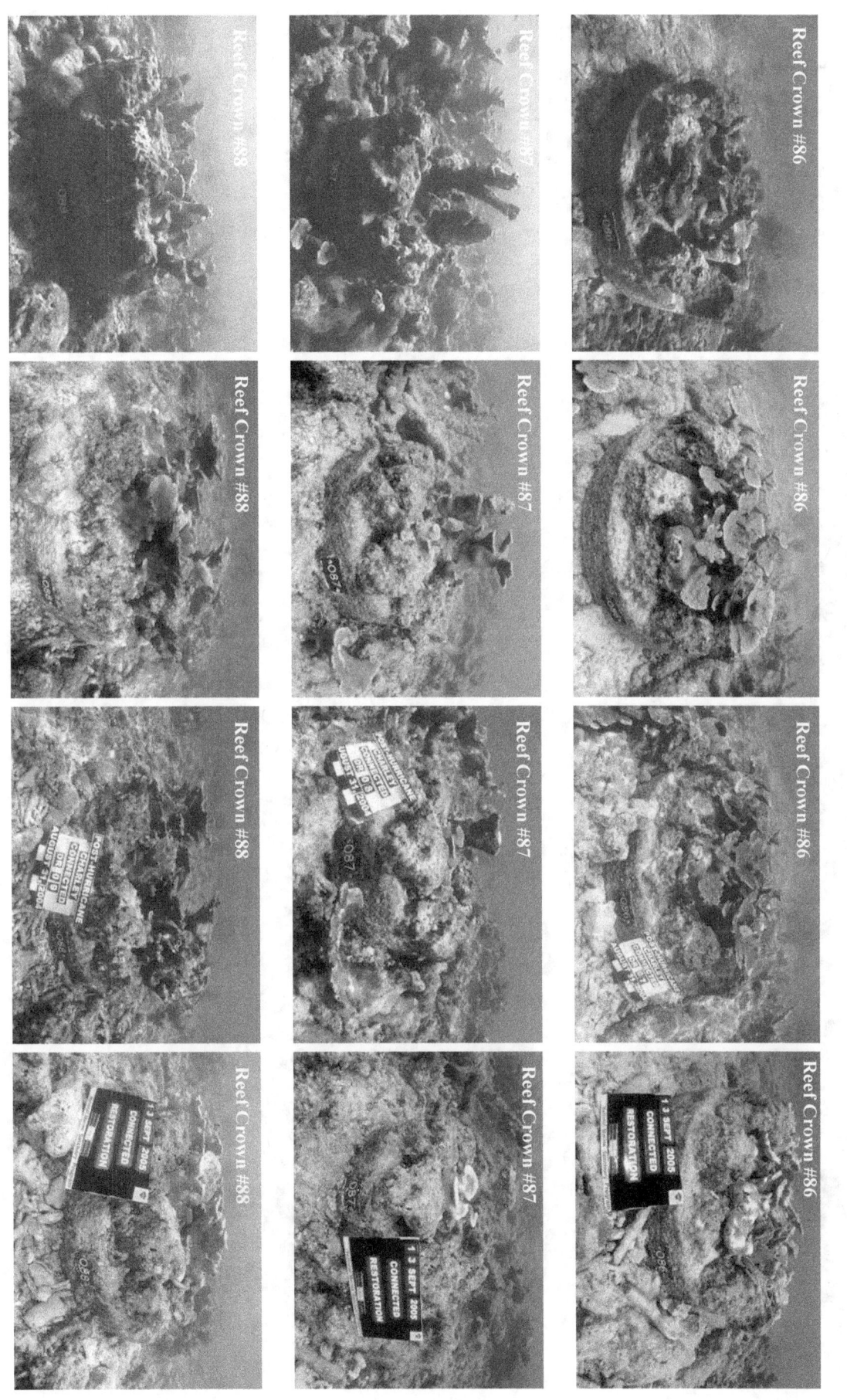

July 19, 2001

July 12, 2004

August 31, 2004

September 13, 2005

Reef Crown #86

Reef Crown #87

Reef Crown #88

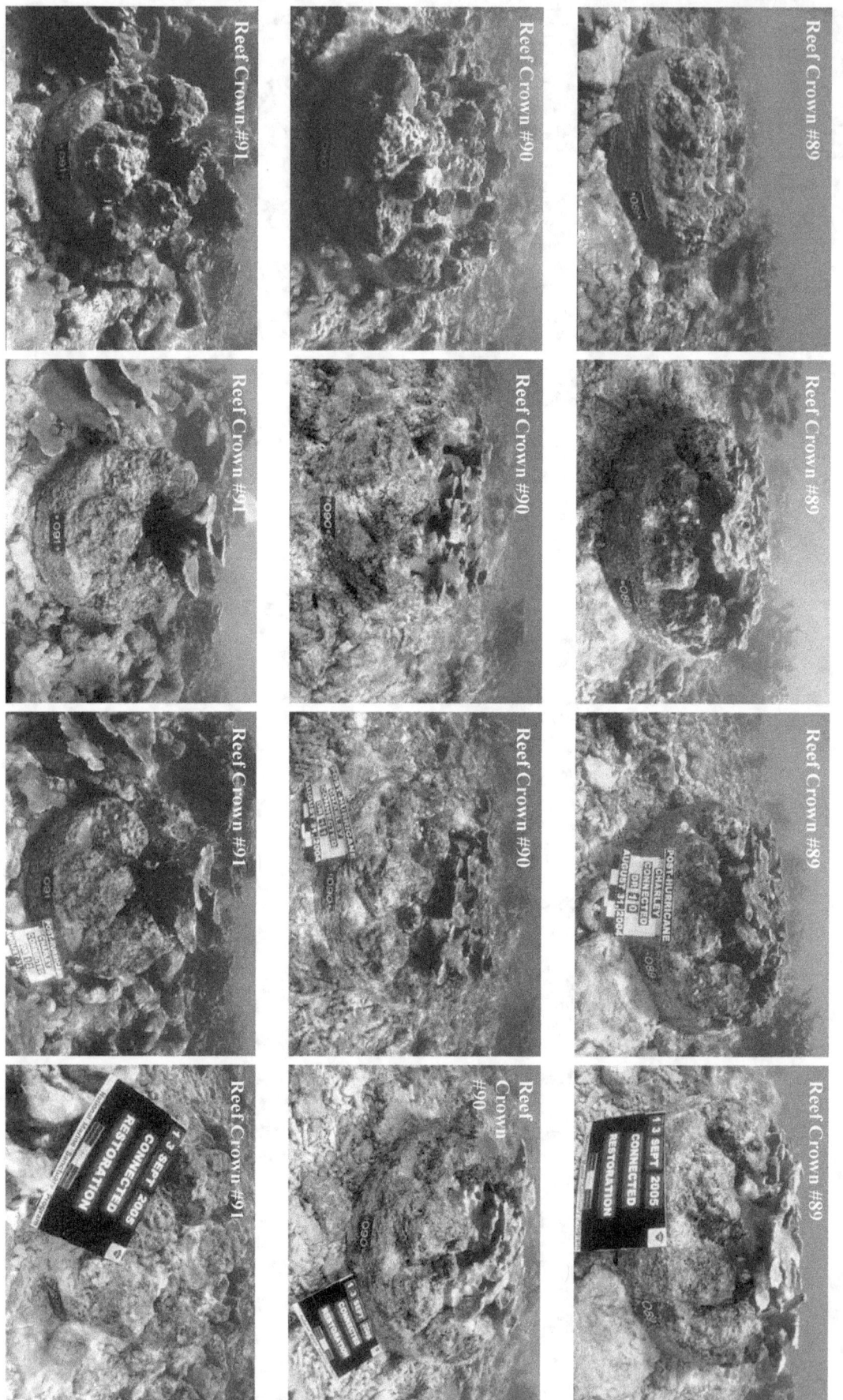

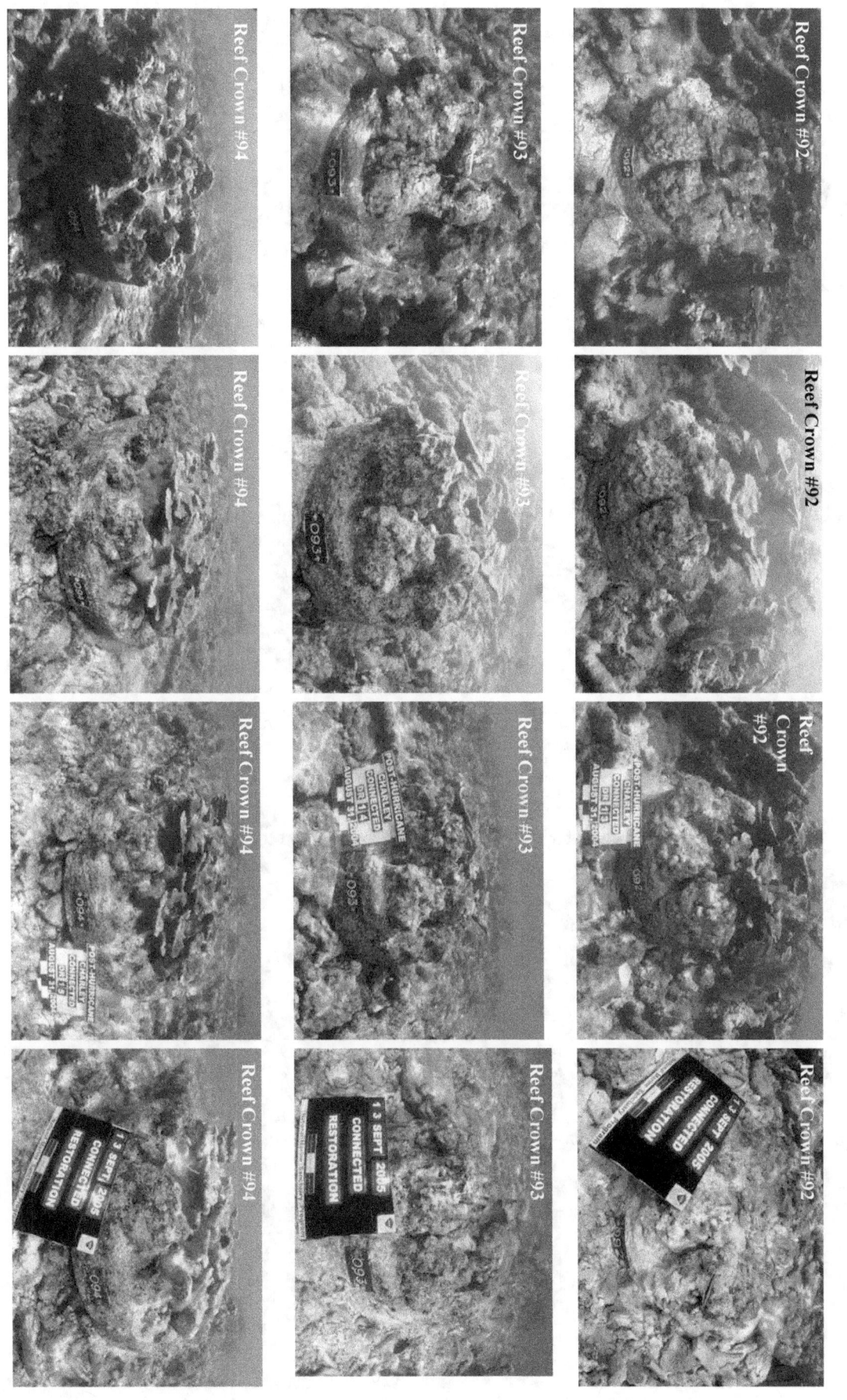

Reef Crown #97   Reef Crown #96   Reef Crown #95   July 19, 2001

Reef Crown #97   Reef Crown #96   Reef Crown #95   July 12, 2004

Reef Crown #97   Reef Crown #96   Reef Crown #95   August 31, 2004

Reef Crown #97   Reef Crown #96   Reef Crown #95   September 13, 2005

24

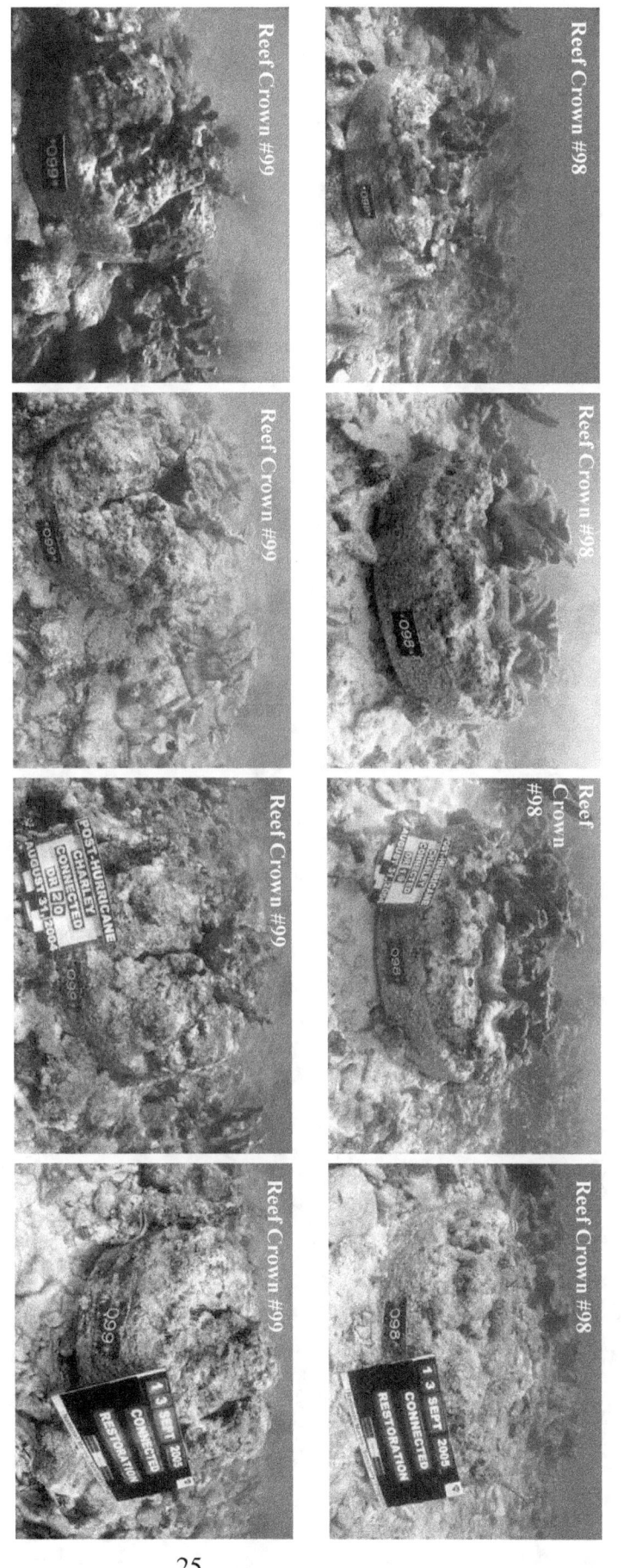

July 19, 2001

July 12, 2004

August 31, 2004

September 13, 2005

25

This page intentionally blank.

NMSP CONSERVATION SERIES PUBLICATIONS

To date, the following reports have been published in the Marine Sanctuaries Conservation Series. All publications are available on the National Marine Sanctuary Program website (http://www.sanctuaries.noaa.gov/).

M/V *JACQUELYN L* Coral Reef Restoration Monitoring Report Monitoring Events 2004-2005 Florida Keys National Marine Sanctuary Monroe County, Florida (NMSP-06-09)

M/V *WAVE WALKER* Coral Reef Restoration Baseline Monitoring Report - 2004 Florida Keys National Marine Sanctuary Monroe County, Florida (NMSP-06-08)

Olympic Coast National Marine Sanctuary Habitat Mapping: Survey report and classification of side scan sonar data from surveys HMPR-114-2004-02 and HMPR-116-2005-01 (NMSP-06-07)

A Pilot Study of Hogfish (*Lachnolaimus maximus* Walbaum 1792) Movement in the Conch Reef Research Only Area (Northern Florida Keys) (NMSP-06-06)

Comments on Hydrographic and Topographic LIDAR Acquisition and Merging with Multibeam Sounding Data Acquired in the Olympic Coast National Marine Sanctuary (ONMS-06-05)

Conservation Science in NOAA's National Marine Sanctuaries: Description and Recent Accomplishments (ONMS-06-04)

Normalization and characterization of multibeam backscatter: Koitlah Point to Point of the Arches, Olympic Coast National Marine Sanctuary - Survey HMPR-115-2004-03 (ONMS-06-03)

Developing Alternatives for Optimal Representation of Seafloor Habitats and Associated Communities in Stellwagen Bank National Marine Sanctuary (ONMS-06-02)

Benthic Habitat Mapping in the Olympic Coast National Marine Sanctuary (ONMS-06-01)

Channel Islands Deep Water Monitoring Plan Development Workshop Report (ONMS-05-05)

Movement of yellowtail snapper (Ocyurus chrysurus Block 1790) and black grouper (Mycteroperca bonaci Poey 1860) in the northern Florida Keys National Marine Sanctuary as determined by acoustic telemetry (MSD-05-4)

The Impacts of Coastal Protection Structures in California's Monterey Bay National Marine Sanctuary (MSD-05-3)

An annotated bibliography of diet studies of fish of the southeast United States and Gray's Reef National Marine Sanctuary (MSD-05-2)

Noise Levels and Sources in the Stellwagen Bank National Marine Sanctuary and the St. Lawrence River Estuary (MSD-05-1)

Biogeographic Analysis of the Tortugas Ecological Reserve (MSD-04-1)

A Review of the Ecological Effectiveness of Subtidal Marine Reserves in Central California (MSD-04-2, MSD-04-3)

Pre-Construction Coral Survey of the M/V Wellwood Grounding Site (MSD-03-1)

Olympic Coast National Marine Sanctuary: Proceedings of the 1998 Research Workshop, Seattle, Washington (MSD-01-04)

Workshop on Marine Mammal Research & Monitoring in the National Marine Sanctuaries (MSD-01-03)

A Review of Marine Zones in the Monterey Bay National Marine Sanctuary (MSD-01-2)

Distribution and Sighting Frequency of Reef Fishes in the Florida Keys National Marine Sanctuary (MSD-01-1)

Flower Garden Banks National Marine Sanctuary: A Rapid Assessment of Coral, Fish, and Algae Using the AGRRA Protocol (MSD-00-3)

The Economic Contribution of Whalewatching to Regional Economies: Perspectives From Two National Marine Sanctuaries (MSD-00-2)

Olympic Coast National Marine Sanctuary Area to be Avoided Education and Monitoring Program (MSD-00-1)

Multi-species and Multi-interest Management: an Ecosystem Approach to Market Squid (*Loligo opalescens*) Harvest in California (MSD-99-1)

www.ingramcontent.com/pod-product-compliance
Lightning Source LLC
Chambersburg PA
CBHW080350290526

45791CB00009BA/2812